NATIONAL GEOGRAPHIC | **CENGAGE**
LEARNING

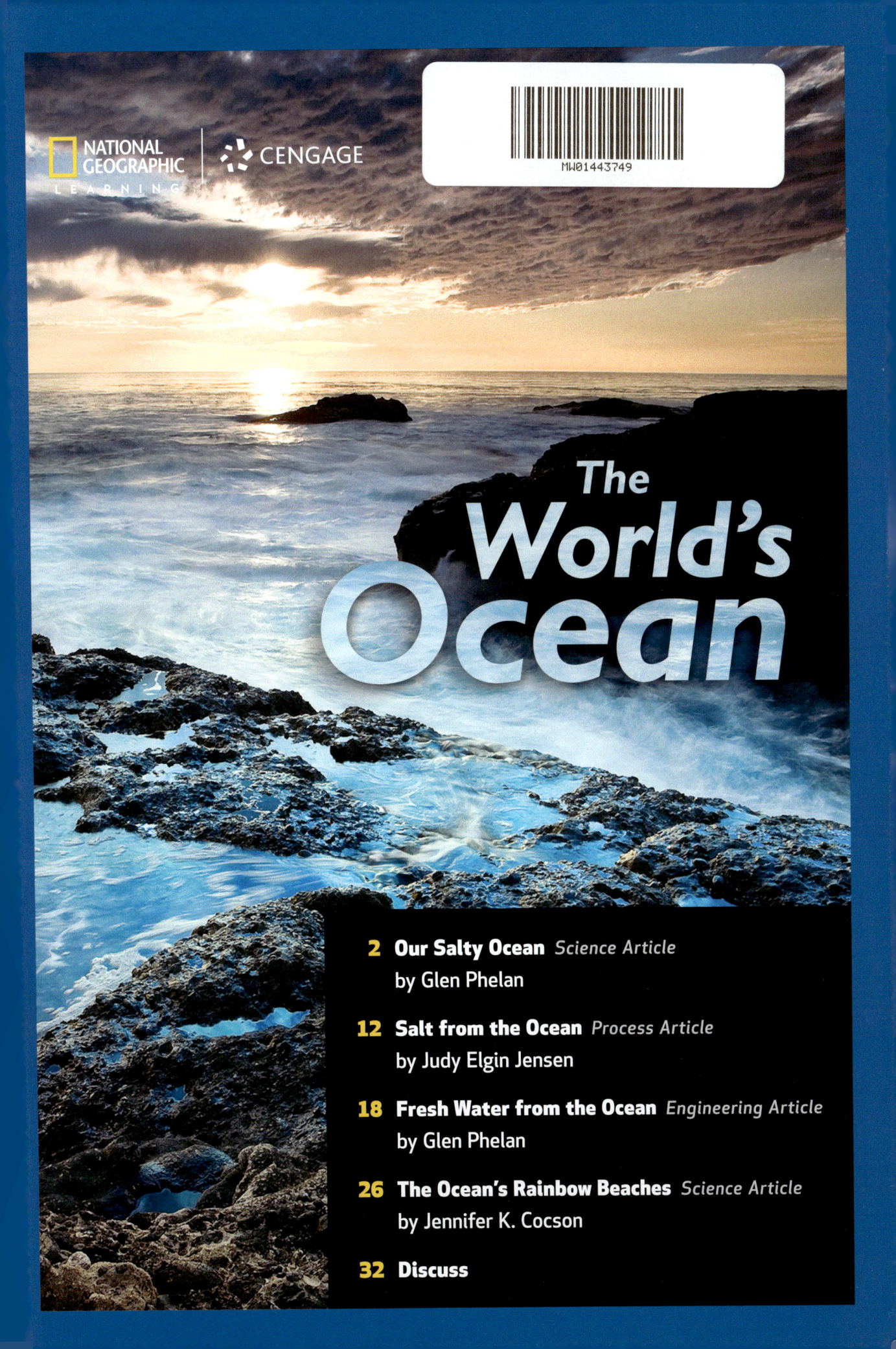

The World's Ocean

2 **Our Salty Ocean** *Science Article*
by Glen Phelan

12 **Salt from the Ocean** *Process Article*
by Judy Elgin Jensen

18 **Fresh Water from the Ocean** *Engineering Article*
by Glen Phelan

26 **The Ocean's Rainbow Beaches** *Science Article*
by Jennifer K. Cocson

32 **Discuss**

GENRE Science Article   Read to find out about properties of the vast world ocean.

Our Salt

Imagine standing on a beach and looking out to sea. The water stretches as far as your eyes can see. Yet this is only a tiny fraction of Earth's global ocean.

The continents separate the ocean into the Arctic, Atlantic, Pacific, and Indian Oceans. However, they are all connected into one ocean. The ocean is full of life, mystery, and surprises.

Earth's "tallest mountain" honor goes to . . . Hawai'i's Mauna Kea. Although it is mostly underwater, it is actually taller than Mount Everest.

10,200m (33,465 ft.)

8,848m (29,028 ft.)

Most of the ocean is so deep that the sun's light cannot reach its depths. Angler fish that live in this darkness have glowing lures that attract prey.

2

y Ocean

by Glen Phelan

Ocean water supports the huge mass of the blue whale. Earth's largest animal ever, it stretches to a length of about 2.5 school buses.

A milk jug's volume of ocean water contains 9 large spoonfuls of salt.

3

Salt Water

Have you ever gone swimming in the ocean? If so, you've probably tasted salty seawater on your lips. Ocean water is mostly a **mixture** of water and different kinds of salts. The salts **dissolve** or break up into particles that spread evenly throughout the water. This makes salt water a kind of mixture called a **solution**. How much salt is in the ocean? Spread evenly over the continents, the salts would form a layer 150 meters (500 feet) thick. That's about the height of a 40-story building.

So how do the salts enter the ocean? Most of the salts come from the land. All natural water has some salts in it. Rain dissolves salts from rocks and soil and washes them into streams. The streams flow into rivers that empty into the ocean. Salts also enter the ocean from volcanoes and small vents on the ocean floor.

Some parts of the global ocean are saltier than others. In the cold polar regions, some ocean water freezes into ice. The ice is made of fresh water. Salt stays behind in the liquid water, making the water around the ice saltier than other parts of the ocean. In the hot tropics, the warm air causes ocean water to **evaporate**. The evaporated water becomes a gas. The salt stays behind in the liquid water. So this part of the ocean is saltier than the rest of the ocean.

Now imagine what happens when fresh river water empties into the ocean. The large amount of fresh water dilutes the saltier ocean water near the mouth of the river. So that small part of the ocean is less salty than other parts.

Ice floats in water, but not right on top! Like an ice cube, most of an iceberg floats below the surface.

water line →

Close to 50,000 icebergs can be seen each year in the Arctic Ocean.

A river in Norway dumps its silt, water, and dissolved salts into a sea that is part of the Arctic Ocean. The silt, or eroded land, forms the fan shape called a delta. The water and dissolved salts mix into the ocean.

Waves

"WATCH OUT!"

A giant wave crashes down upon a surfer. It looks like a wipeout for sure. Then, seconds later, the surfer emerges and rides the wave to shore.

Surfers know all about waves. Most waves are caused by wind, or moving air. The blowing winds drag across the surface and pass energy to the water.

In 2012, a surfer rode a record-breaking 24-meter (78-foot) wave off the coast of Nazaré, Portugal.

The wind's energy passes through the water as waves. The stronger the winds are, the bigger the waves are. Imagine a storm at sea. Fierce winds kick up some serious waves. The energy might take many hours to reach the coast. When it does, the waves can be taller than houses.

Now imagine that you're on your surfboard. You bob up and down as the waves roll past you. The wave moves forward. But the water, and you, just bob up and down.

You spot a good wave coming. You paddle forward and then stand up as the water swells beneath your board. It's a nice-sized wave, about half your height, but that's about to change.

The wave has grown and now towers over you. What's going on? The water is shallow enough that the bottom of the wave rubs against the ocean floor. This slows the wave but also pushes it higher.

You can feel the wave breaking! The bottom of the wave slows down more than the top does, so the top leans forward, curls, and topples over. That's about the only time that a wave actually pushes water forward. It pushes you forward too, but you keep your balance. What a fantastic ride!

Sea stars, barnacles, and other tide pool organisms can live both in and out of water.

Nearly 4,000 kinds of fish dart and glide among the reefs of the ocean.

Animals in the open ocean swim for miles in search of food.

Ocean Life

Earth's ocean is home to organisms of every color, shape, and size. Whales, dolphins, octopuses, and fish are swimmers. Lobsters, corals, and sea stars are bottom dwellers that live on the ocean floor. Jellies are floaters, staying near the surface.

All ocean organisms are adapted to life in the ocean's salty water. For example, having too much salt in a fish's body can be harmful. So fish pass extra salt through their skin and gills.

There are many ocean environments, each with its own unique mix of life. Tide pools are rocky depressions along shore. They are underwater during high tide and stay filled with water during low tide. The watery solution in tide pools becomes more salty as water evaporates. It becomes less salty when the tide comes in or when it rains.

The greatest variety of ocean life is found on or near coral reefs. Tiny animals called corals make limestone coverings that build the stony reefs.

Some reef visitors, such as sharks and dolphins, are more at home in the open ocean. Compare the organisms that live in the environments shown here. These are just a few of the living things found in the world's salty ocean.

A mouthful of seawater can contain hundreds of thousands of tiny animals and plantlike organisms. Millions of bacteria live there, too. Spit it out!

In the Deep

In 1977, a scientist and a pilot slowly descended into the Pacific Ocean. They were in a small research submarine called *Alvin*. Another scientist kept track of *Alvin* from the mother ship on the surface. Their goal was to find out if some of the ocean's salt was coming from volcanic vents on the seafloor. No one had ever explored these vents. These scientists made the discovery of a lifetime.

As *Alvin* neared the ocean floor, the pilot called out, "There's clams out here!" The giant clams were each bigger than a football. There were also anemones, crabs, mussels, fish, and gigantic worms that were taller than a doorway. The worms had red tips that came out of thin white tubes.

One of the scientists later described the worms to her colleagues. "I asked, 'Hey, can you biologists tell us what these things are?' And they said, 'What? We don't know what that is. Hold everything!'"

The scientists had discovered creatures living in total darkness. Without sunlight, how did the organisms get energy?

The nearby vents release a mixture of salts, minerals, chemical gases, and extremely hot water. One of these gases is food for bacteria that live inside certain animals. The bacteria use the gas to make chemicals that the animals use as food.

Since 1977, scientists have discovered many vents and the life around them. *Alvin* and other high-tech tools continue to explore the ocean. Maybe one day, you'll make a discovery on a deep-sea voyage.

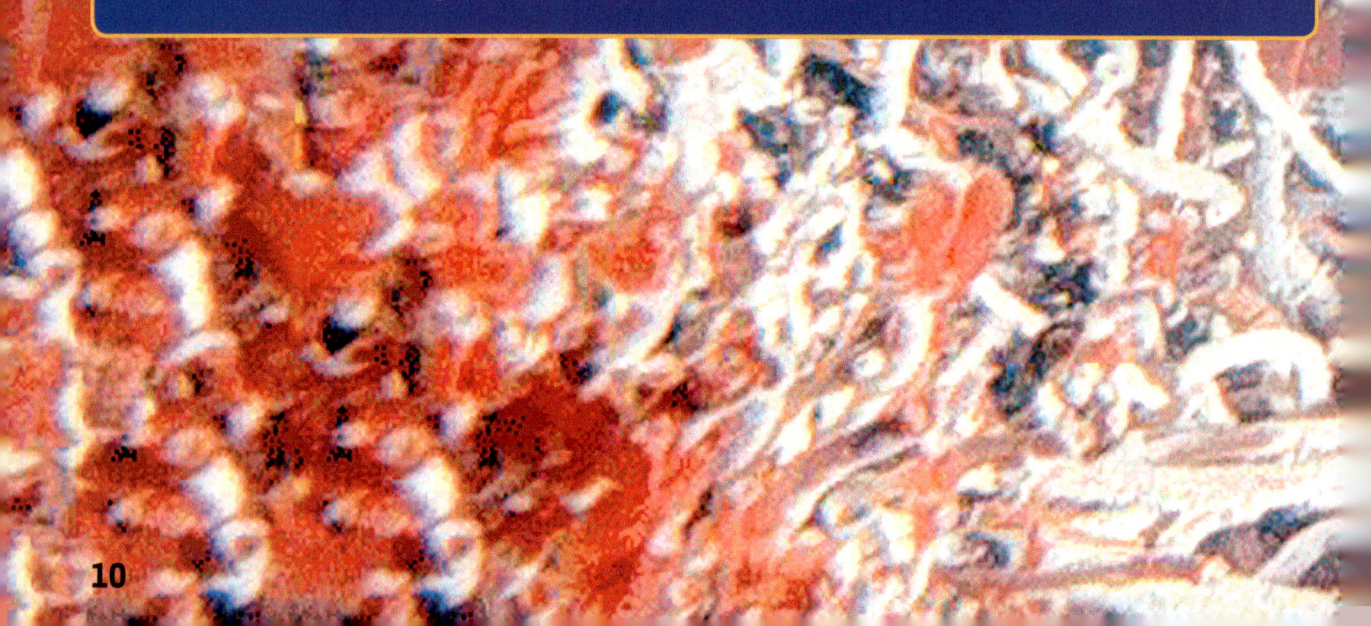

The black plumes, rich in chemicals such as sulfur, iron, zinc, and copper, measure over 350°C (662°F)!

The bright light shining on these strange animals comes from the submarine.

Check In Why are some parts of the ocean saltier than others?

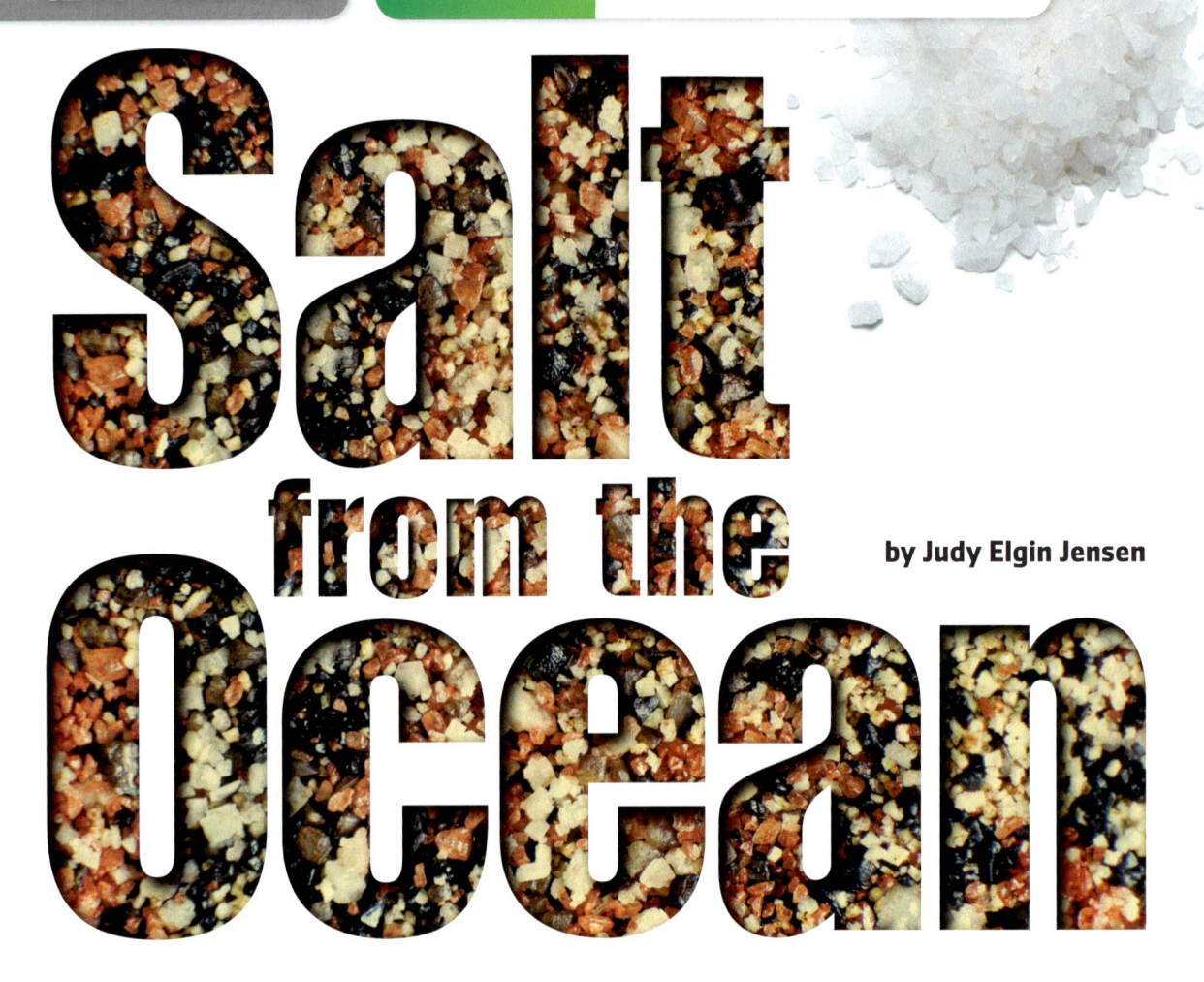

GENRE Process Article   **Read to find out** how salt is harvested from the ocean.

Salt from the Ocean

by Judy Elgin Jensen

When you reach for a saltshaker in a restaurant, you might pick up a container labeled "sea salt." What exactly is sea salt?

Sea salt is salt that comes from the sea, or ocean. Seawater **evaporates** from shallow pools. The salt that is left behind is harvested. Table salt comes from underground mines.

Table salt and sea salt are not that different. Both salts are made of sodium chloride. Many sea salts are left in large grains. You can use a grinder to break the grains apart. Sea salt also has minerals that give the salt different flavors and colors. You can use these different salts to enhance your food. Here are just a few kinds of sea salts available today.

Fleur de Sel That's French for "Flower of Salt." It's the best of the salt harvested in certain regions of France.

Black Lava Sea Salt This salt is produced on the Hawaiian island of Moloka'i. It is rich in minerals and has a nutty flavor. Charcoal gives it its color.

Chipotle Sea Salt Pacific sea salt is mixed with smoke-dried chipotle peppers to give this salt a spicy kick.

Red Alaea Sea Salt Red clay from Hawai'i gives this Pacific sea salt its color. It is rich in minerals and is used to flavor and preserve food.

French Grey Sea Salt This coarse salt is harvested from the Atlantic waters near France. It smells like the ocean and is rich in minerals.

Apple Smoked Salt This fruity salt is slowly smoked over a fire burning wood from apple trees. It also contains minerals from the sea water.

Harvesting Sea Salt

Life in the ocean needs salt water to survive. People need some salt, too. A lot of the salt we use comes from the evaporation of salty seawater.

Sea salt is harvested in warm climates where the breezes are strong and steady. And of course, seawater must be nearby and plentiful.

The photos of these salt ponds show steps in the process of harvesting sea salt on the island of Gozo, Malta, in the Mediterranean Sea. Let's see how it's done.

Step 1

First, seawater is pumped into shallow ponds that are made of local clay. Wind and sunlight slowly evaporate the water. The remaining **solution**, called **brine**, gets saltier as more water evaporates.

Step 2

The brine moves through a series of ponds over time. After almost two years, solid salt crystals start forming in the briny solution.

Step 3

Evaporation continues and more salt crystals form in the brine. When the salt layer is about 10 centimeters (4 inches) thick, the salt is broken up, scooped, and taken to the wash plant.

Step 4

At the wash plant, the salt is cleaned and stored. It is then crushed, dried, and packaged. Then it's off to the store!

Importance of Salt

Salt is much more than a seasoning. Entire civilizations have been impacted by it. For example, in the late 1500s, salt helped the Dutch avoid war with Spain. The Dutch stopped one of Spain's most important salt plants from transporting salt. Unable to sell their salt, Spain did not have the money to fight a war.

▼ A scale for measuring sea salt is a common tool at open-air markets. This market is in East Timor on an island north of Australia.

Sacks of local sea salts are on sale at a market on the Spanish island of Mallorca in the Mediterranean Sea.

Over the years, salt has been used as money. Soldiers of ancient Rome were paid partly in salt. In fact, the word *salary* comes from the Latin word for "salt."

How have these tiny crystals had so much power? Your body needs salt, though in small amounts. Salt helps your muscles work, your blood flow, and your heart beat. It also slows the growth of bacteria that spoil food. Salting was an important way to preserve fish and meats before refrigeration existed. Salting continues in many cultures today.

Sea salt has once again become important to many local economies. A small sea salt works in Maine evaporates seawater in solar greenhouses to produce salt. A huge sea salt works outside San Francisco looks similar to others around the world. Merchants compete for customers as the sea salt trend grows.

A crust of salt kept these fish from spoiling. They will be grilled and sold at a market in Bangkok, Thailand.

Check In Why is seawater pumped into shallow ponds rather than deep ponds?

GENRE Engineering Article **Read to find out** about a solution to a freshwater supply problem.

Fresh Water from the Ocean

by Glen Phelan

EARLY DUBAI, 60 YEARS AGO

The dust is everywhere. It gets in your clothing, your hair, your eyes. Meanwhile, the sun is blazing and temperatures are soaring.

That's just the way it is here in the Middle Eastern city of Dubai. After all, this *is* a desert. This is a poor town where most people cannot read or write. Jobs are few.

Children play with balls made of rags. Many people live in tents and barely make a living fishing for sardines in the Persian Gulf.

You turn the corner and come nose-to-nose with a camel. Its owner uses the animal to carry goods to one of Dubai's open-air markets. You smell the sweet aromas of cinnamon and cloves and listen to people arguing over prices. Then you continue on your way.

A few minutes later you come to a small saltwater creek. It empties into the Persian Gulf, which is salt water too. Little rain falls. There are no rivers and no big lakes to supply fresh water either. So where do people get drinking water? A few deep wells provide water for the 30,000 people who live here. Yet fresh water is a scarce resource.

A saltwater creek divides the city. Everywhere else is dry, desert sand.

DUBAI, TODAY

Now you are in the largest mall in the world, right here in Dubai. Pop music blares. Some people wear traditional Arabic clothing while others wear shorts and jeans. The Dubai Mall has 1,200 stores, an ice rink, an aquarium, a theme park, and movie theaters. Skyscrapers, including the world's tallest, line wide streets outside. People from all over the world stay in fancy hotels. How did the dusty town become such a sparkling city?

Oil was discovered beneath Dubai's desert sands in the 1960s. It wasn't as much oil as in other parts of the Middle East, but it helped boost Dubai's economy. New wealth led to new businesses. People came to build the modern city and the population grew to more than a million people.

As Dubai grew, it faced a major problem. There was a shortage of fresh water. People needed fresh water for drinking, washing, farming,

Peering up at the gleaming towers of glass and steel, or strolling through an indoor mall, it's hard to imagine the Dubai of 60 years ago.

and running factories. Scientists figured out how to get fresh water from salt water in a process called **desalination**.

What does the word *desalination* mean? The prefix *de-* means "to reverse or remove." The root word *saline* is Latin for "salt." The suffix *-ation* means "result of an action." So desalination is the action of removing salt.

There are several ways to desalinate salt water. Many desalination plants rely on evaporation and condensation. When water **evaporates**, the salt stays behind.

The water that evaporates into water vapor is fresh. Many desalination plants catch this fresh water vapor. They **condense** it, or turn it back into liquid. The condensed water is piped to storage tanks. The Jebel Ali desalination plant in Dubai turns salty seawater from the Persian Gulf into drinkable fresh water.

Farmers in the Liwa Oasis irrigate with groundwater. The oasis is a four-hour drive from Dubai.

USING DESALINATED WATER

In countries in the Middle East, most of the drinking water comes from desalination plants.

Desalinated water is used in many ways. Industries use desalinated water to make products. Some farmers use desalinated water to irrigate fields. Most farmers use **groundwater**, which is water that collects between rocks underground.

Without desalination, cities along the coast would have to pipe groundwater over long distances. If people in the cities used more groundwater, less would be available for crops.

Desalination isn't perfect. It requires lots of energy. Most desalination plants burn fossil fuels to heat the seawater. This creates a lot of pollution. So engineers have designed desalination plants that use solar energy to heat the water.

A lot of salty **brine** is produced through desalination. This can be unhealthy to nearby ocean life. So engineers designed a system in which the brine releases slowly. The brine mixes more safely with the surrounding ocean water.

The water released back into the ocean can be warmer than the surrounding area, too. This warm water can form a layer and trap tiny ocean life below. It also may not have enough oxygen for the ocean organisms to survive. Scientists continue to study problems with desalination and design solutions.

DESALINATION AROUND THE WORLD

Desalination is becoming more and more important. Many Middle Eastern countries rely on desalination for their drinking water. Desalination plants around the world produce 65 billion liters (17 billion gallons) of fresh water every day! That's a lot! Yet that's only about two percent of all the fresh water people use every day. Desalination plants are expensive to run but more of them are being built. Some are used only in times of drought. Others sit far

United Kingdom: London
The plant is powered with biofuel. It runs only in times of drought to supply 1 million people.

United States: Tampa
The plant supplies up to 10 percent of the region's needs. It helps conserve groundwater and reservoir stores.

Chile: Caldera
The plant ensures water needs for mining the rich mineral resources in the Atacama Desert. This desert is the driest location on Earth.

24

inland and extract salt from reservoirs or groundwater supplies that contain water that is too briny to drink.

Technology is improving. This makes desalination more affordable and environmentally friendly. Maybe someday you'll work on technology that will help provide fresh water to a thirsty world.

India: Chennai
The plant supplies 4.5 million people. Water shortages result when erratic monsoons don't fill lakes and reservoirs.

Australia: Melbourne
The plant serves a growing population. Changing rainfall patterns mean reservoir stores can't keep up.

South Africa: Mossel Bay
The plant can supply all of the town's needs in case of a severe drought. Droughts are somewhat common here.

Check In What problems in the desalination process are engineers trying to solve?

GENRE Science Article **Read to find out** why beaches are different colors.

THE OCEAN'S Rainbow Beaches

by Jennifer K. Cocson

Punalu'u Beach

Seawater is a **mixture** of water, salts, minerals, gases, and microscopic life. This watery mixture constantly washes over another mixture, the beach. Yes, a beach is a mixture. Just scoop up a handful and you'll see sand, shells, and pebbles.

Where do these beach ingredients come from? The shells wash up from the ocean while the rocks and sand usually come from the land nearby. Rivers carry **eroded** bits of rock downstream and dump them near the coast. Breaking waves smash rocks against each other. The rocks break into small pieces and eventually turn into grains of sand. The crashing waves also erode, or wear down, the rocky shoreline. The constant motion of the waves forms a beach that is a mixture of the local rocky material.

Beaches come in a rainbow of colors. Let's take a look at some of the world's most colorful beaches.

Hawai'i is famous for its gorgeous beaches. Just look at the black grains of sand on Punalu'u Beach. The grains are tiny bits of hardened lava. Hot lava flows down the volcano that forms the island. It cools as soon as it hits the ocean water and turns into black rock called basalt. Waves pound the basalt into black sand.

The black sand of this beach in Hawai'i comes from the black volcanic rock that makes up much of the island.

What makes the sand at Puʻu Māhana Beach in Hawaiʻi green?

Puʻu Māhana Beach

Now let's travel west to Puʻu Māhana Beach. The sand grains are like tiny green jewels. The olive-green color comes from the mineral olivine.

The cliffs around the beach are the remains of a hill formed by volcanic debris. These cliffs are loaded with olivine. Rain washes bits of olivine down the cliffs. Waves also erode the cliff and wash olivine on shore.

The grains of olivine are too small to be valuable. But larger crystals of olivine are the semi-precious gem called peridot.

Now hop over to Pink Sands Beach in the Bahamas. Can you guess where the pink sand comes from? Tiny animals with bright pink or red shells live among the nearby coral reefs. After the animals die, the waves smash the shells and wash the bits onto the shore. The shells mix in with the white sand to give the beach a pink color.

Pink Sands Beach

The color of Pink Sands Beach in the Bahamas has a surprising source.

Rainbow Beach

Let's end our tour with Rainbow Beach on the east coast of Australia. It's named for the colorful sandy cliffs and dunes behind it. These cliffs and dunes have more than 70 shades of tan, yellow, orange, pink, red, blue, and brown.

A native legend tells of a spirit that took the form of a rainbow. After being killed, the spirit crashed into the cliffs, giving them their rainbow of color. The legend is important to the native culture. However, scientists know that a mixture of different minerals gives the cliffs their colorful layers.

Erosion from wind and waves breaks down the cliffs and forms sand at the base. Wind and waves shift the sand and create an ever-changing colorful beach.

⌄ Look at all that color in the sandy cliffs of Rainbow Beach. How do you think these cliffs affect the appearance of the beach?

⌃ The sandy rainbows at Rainbow Beach in Queensland, Australia change often.

You can see some of Rainbow Beach's colorful sands on the surface. But as you dig into the sand, you can see new colors with each scoop!

The next time you are at a beach, observe what makes up this sandy mixture. Try to figure out where the components of the mixture came from. Are there hills and cliffs nearby? What are the rocks like? What kind of minerals do they contain?

Look at a map. Does a river empty into the ocean or lake close by? What kind of land did the river flow through on its long journey here?

Whew! Those are a lot of questions. Searching for the answers is where the adventure begins!

Check In How can you predict the color of a beach by looking at the nearby landforms?

Discuss

1. Tell about some of the ways you think the four pieces in *The World's Ocean* are connected.

2. Think about the process of getting salt from the ocean described in "Salt from the Ocean" and the process of getting fresh water described in "Fresh Water from the Ocean." Identify the cause and effect in each one.

3. Explain how the physical properties of the surrounding rocks and soils impact salt in "Salt from the Ocean" and sand in "Rainbow Beaches."

4. Cite evidence from "Our Salty Ocean" for why salinity varies in locations around the world.

5. What questions do you still have about the world's ocean? What would be some good ways to find out more information?